Killers On The Grassy Lands ~ East African Bullfrog
Written and Illustrated by Jeff Terry

The mouth of an East African Bullfrog can widen up to the size of its head and fire its tongue at its prey.

Its front feet can stuff its prey into its mouth after pinning it to the ground.

Its back feet can shovel away soil for burrowing.

Its eyes can plunge its prey down its throat.

Its vocal pouch can balloon up when croaking.

Its eardrums can spring off sound.

Its skin can sweat mucus to keep it nice and moist.

Its tongue can whip its flying prey out of the air and reel it into its mouth.

Its fingers and toes can poke the ground.

Its back legs can catapult its body high in the air.

Its main prey are insects but it can also gobble up mice and its own kind.

Jeff Terry enjoys drawing, reading and writing about animals and sculpting with clay.
"With God all things are possible." Matthew 19:26

Manufactured by Amazon.ca
Bolton, ON

14656972R00017